Tell Me WHY

BODY

Questions and Answers

by

Rebecca Phillips-Bartlett

Minneapolis, Minnesota

Credits
All images are courtesy of Shutterstock.com, unless otherwise specified. With thanks to Getty Images, Thinkstock Photo, and iStockphoto.

Cover – BNP Design Studio, Guz Anna, katoten, mentalmind. Throughout – BNP Design Studio. 4 – Colorfuel Studio, monkeybusinessimages. 5 – Magorzata 6&7 – SharkPaeCNX, ianakauri, Evgeny Atamanenko, Guz Anna, wickerwood, Vera Larina. 8 – PaulGregg. 10&11 – khosrork, mentalmind, Yavdat, svtdesign. 12&13 – Onica Alexandru Sergiu, Alexander_Safonov, wissanustock. 14 – Bohdan Malitskiy 15 – khuruzero, StoryTime Studio, mayalis. 17 – Jasen Wright. 18&19 – Colorfuel Studio, Nikolai Moiseenko. 20 – Tenstudio, wusuowei. 22 – Potapov Alexander. 23 – pixologicstudio

Bearport Publishing Company Product Development Team
President: Jen Jenson; Director of Product Development: Spencer Brinker; Managing Editor: Allison Juda; Associate Editor: Naomi Reich; Associate Editor: Tiana Tran; Art Director: Colin O'Dea; Designer: Elena Klinkner; Designer: Kayla Eggert; Product Development Assistant: Owen Hamlin

Library of Congress Cataloging-in-Publication Data is available at www.loc.gov or upon request from the publisher.

ISBN: 979-8-88916-393-0 (hardcover)
ISBN: 979-8-88916-398-5 (paperback)
ISBN: 979-8-88916-402-9 (ebook)

For more information, write to Bearport Publishing, 5357 Penn Avenue South, Minneapolis, MN 55419.

Contents

TELL ME WHY

We use our bodies to run, laugh, and play with friends. But they also work hard to keep us alive and healthy.

QUESTION
What questions do you have about your body?

Our bodies can do many things all on their own, such as breathing and sneezing. We don't see all of the interesting things they do. Sometimes, this can leave us wondering **WHY?**

WHY CAN'T I TICKLE MYSELF?

Tickling works best when it is a surprise. But it is hard to surprise yourself. When you try to tickle yourself, your brain knows what to expect and prepares for it. That's why others can tickle you but you can't tickle yourself.

FUN FACT

The only place most people can tickle themselves is the roof of their mouth.

WHY DO MY FINGERS GET WRINKLY IN WATER?

When you get into the water, your body sends less blood to your hands. This causes the skin to become loose and wrinkly. Scientists believe your body does this to give you extra **grip** when your hands are wet.

FUN FACT

Humans and macaque monkeys are the only animals that get wrinkly in water.

WHY DO I CLOSE MY EYES WHEN I SNEEZE?

Your eyes squeeze shut every time you have a big sneeze. You don't even think about it happening. Scientists aren't completely sure why our eyes close, but they have some ideas.

A sneeze is one way your body gets rid of **germs**. Your eyes might close to stop the germs from getting back into your body.

Another reason could be because of **muscles**. When you sneeze, the muscles in your face **contract**, or tighten up. This may force your eyes to close.

QUESTION

Which do you think is the more likely reason?

WHY DOES MY STOMACH GROWL?

Your stomach has muscles to move food through your body. It does this by squeezing. If it's been a while since you have eaten, there's nothing to muffle the sounds of your stomach squeezing.

WHY DO PEOPLE LIKE DIFFERENT FOODS?

The same food will taste different to every person. This is because we all have different taste buds. Some people have more of these little bumps on their tongues. The more you have, the stronger something might taste.

FUN FACT

People with lots of taste buds are called supertasters.

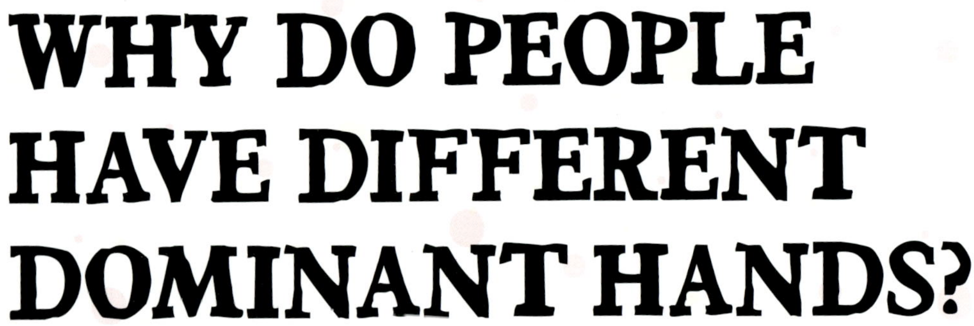

WHY DO PEOPLE HAVE DIFFERENT DOMINANT HANDS?

Your brain has two sides. The right half controls the left side of your body, and the left half of your brain controls the right side. Some scientists think your **dominant** hand is based on which side of your brain is stronger.

WHY DO MY TEETH FALL OUT?

It's perfectly normal for your baby teeth to fall out. These smaller teeth are just keeping space ready for your adult teeth! As you grow and get bigger, there is more room in your mouth for your adult teeth to fit.

WHY DO I GET HICCUPS?

A muscle called the **diaphragm** helps you breathe. It pulls air in and out of your lungs. Sometimes, the diaphragm twitches and makes you suck in air quickly. The blast of air can make part of your throat close up, which causes the silly hiccup sound.

WHY DOES MY HEAD HURT WHEN I EAT ICE CREAM TOO QUICKLY?

This is known as a brain freeze. When something really cold touches the roof of your mouth, your body tries to warm it back up. It makes the **blood vessels** in your head open wider to let more blood in. This quick change can sometimes hurt.

WHY IS HAIR DIFFERENT COLORS?

FUN FACT
Melanin is the same thing that gives people different skin colors, too.

Hair gets its color from something called **melanin**. The more melanin someone's hair has, the darker it will be. So, people with blond or red hair have less melanin, and people with brown or black hair have more.

WHY DOES HAIR GO GRAY?

As people get older, their bodies make less melanin. Hair won't have as much color as it grows. When this happens, hair starts to look gray, silver, or white.

FUN FACT

There are stories about people's hair turning gray overnight. Scientists don't believe this can really happen.

WHY DO I YAWN?

Scientists aren't completely sure why we yawn, but they have a few ideas. Your brain works best at a certain **temperature**. When you yawn, your body takes in large amounts of cool air. This could help cool down your brain.

FUN FACT

Most people yawn more during the winter than the summer.

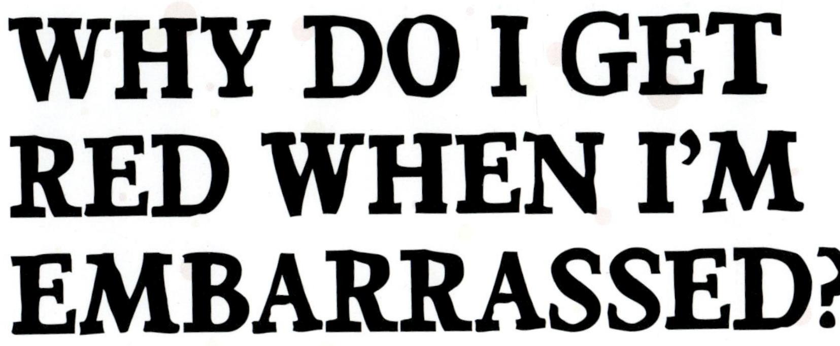

WHY DO I GET RED WHEN I'M EMBARRASSED?

When you get **embarrassed**, your body gets ready to run away. To do this, your body needs to move lots of blood around. The blood gets closer to your skin, making your face and the rest of your body look red.

WHY DO I DREAM?

Nobody is really sure why we dream, but scientists believe dreams can be helpful. Dreaming about things that have happened can help make your memory better. Scientists think it may even make you more creative.

WHY DO I HAVE BAD DREAMS?

Some people think even bad dreams can be helpful, too. Although dreams aren't real, they bring up very real feelings. This can allow us to work to understand and deal with those feelings when we are awake.

Asking Questions

Asking questions is a great way to learn about everything from your nose to your toes. Just like you, scientists still have a lot of questions about our bodies.

There is still plenty to discover about the interesting things our bodies do. So, stay curious, and keep asking questions!

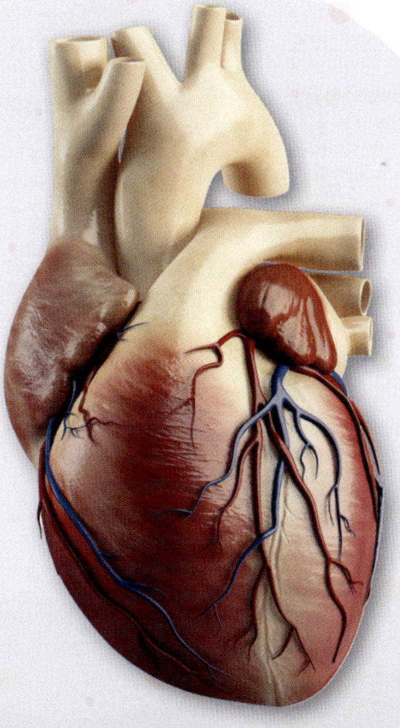

QUESTION

What are other questions you have about your body?

Glossary

blood vessels tiny tubes that carry blood around a person's body

contract to tighten or become smaller

diaphragm a muscle in the lower chest that is used to breathe

dominant the most powerful or strongest

embarrassed feeling confused or silly in front of others

germs tiny living things that can cause illnesses

grip a strong hold on something

melanin a substance that creates color in the hair and skin

muscles parts of the body that are used for movement

temperature how hot or cold something is

Index